The Three Paths to Healing

How Your Deepest Wound Can Guide You
to Craft a Monumental Life

Dominic Mitges

The Three Paths to Healing: How Your Deepest Wound Can Guide You to Create a Monumental Life, by Dominic Mitges

Layout and Design:
One Thousand Trees
www.onethousandtrees.com

Table of Contents

Introduction

Within this book lie the lessons that I have taken and internalized from the most traumatic experiences of my life. I have encountered the unspeakable on more than one occasion. So I have been where you are. I have been dead inside, numb, void of purpose, meaning, fulfillment, and the desire to continue along the path. Many have quit; but not me. And not you either. You and I are here to do amazing things.

I've come to understand that those of us who have been through the deepest, darkest pain are the ones who have the most to offer our world. Those who have endured the most are those who can access the most. It will be us who transform our world. We need you and people like you now more than ever. Our world is hurting. There is a place for you here.

Do not make the mistake of judging this book's value by its size. I wanted to write a book that was compact with impact. I want to deliver the wisdom without the unnecessary filler that so many books include. I want to deliver the wisdom with context. Nothing more.

I have come to realize there are 3 stages of healing one goes through on the path to wholeness. These stages are Guided Healing, Self-Healing, and Healing Ourselves Through Healing Others. It is important to keep in mind that the 3 Paths of Healing are not separate from one another. In the western world, we always seem to want a program that takes us incrementally from step 1 to step 2 to step 3 and we are done. We tend towards very linear thinking.

The healing process never works this way, though. Going through my own healing and guiding countless individuals through theirs, I have found each of these paths work together, sometimes all at the same time! So this is not a rigid program you must adhere to. Healing is so individual; there is no one size fits all and there never will be.

The experiences and beliefs I share in this book are exactly that. Yes, they have helped some people, and others did not connect with it. That's ok. I do not fall prey to the illusion that my way is *the* way or the *right* way. My way is just *one* way. I am not here to fix you, I am here as a catalyst for healing; a stepping-stone along your path.

My goal with this book is to model possibility for you. You are not alone, and you are not "bad" or "crazy." I want to show you that no matter who you are, where you are, or what you have been through, there is always a way out. There is always something bigger, better, and more fulfilling waiting for you just on the other side of whatever you're going through. I am here to show you how to do so because I know you can. Because I love you and I believe in you, even if you don't yet believe in yourself.

And because I once was you, and I am now who you can be.

I believe in you,

Dominic Mitges

The First Path: Guided Healing

So the first stage is Guided Healing. This step takes place when we become consciously aware there is a dis-ease in our minds and bodies and we feel we cannot handle what we are going through alone so we reach out for help. This help could come in the form of a mental health professional, a peer who has experienced something similar and has made great strides in their own healing, a coach, a spiritual advisor, and so on. Often, the person in this stage has made some initial yet sometimes counterproductive attempts to self-heal (through denial of feelings, substance abuse, food, distracting themselves with seemingly "harmless" pastimes like social media, television, video and computer games, etc.

Not only are these counterproductive, but they also tend to prolong the healing process and amplify the pain. Especially in the case of those who have developed addictions: it is incredibly difficult if not impossible to heal what we are trying to escape through the addiction without first addressing the addiction. The person must take the painful steps to acknowledge their addiction and deal with the physical, emotional, mental and spiritual symptoms of withdrawal from whatever substance they're taking before they can truly be present to address the underlying issues.

Other times, the person has done some serious introspection and made great strides alone, but needs help integrating them. Usually, guided healing involves self-healing as well because the real work is done after the person guiding the healing sessions has helped the person being healed come to some pretty stark realizations about themselves and their past. It's usually between these sessions that the person does the work necessary to progress through introspection and deeper exploration of what was raised with the healer. As I stated, these processes are not linear and often we will go through these stages several times as we heal and grow and journey deeper into ourselves.

One of the reasons Guided Healing can be so effective is because it provides us with a new perspective. Our perspective of a particular situation determines how we feel about it and how we deal with it. For example, when I was depressed and guilt-ridden over my father's suicide, my perspective caused me to withdraw, engage in destructive internal dialogue, and subconsciously sabotage my relationships and my work. My perspective on the situation was I didn't do enough to help him and so I didn't deserve anything good to manifest for me. I believed I was undeserving of every measure of success in life, including love, so that affected my mind, which affected how I showed up in the world.

Years later, however, after having done the deep, sometimes painful work needed to fully process and discharge the guilt, shame, and pain of the situation, my perspective has changed.

The result has been due in part to my experience with Guided Healing; working with a spiritual counselor, yoga and meditation teachers, reading the great spiritual and psychological works, as well as learning everything I could about suicide and the psychology behind it through suicide prevention and awareness courses.

Working with various teachers, counselors, and healers has made me realize that we get so stuck in one perspective we believe it is the only one through which to view the situation. This couldn't be further from the truth. Every one I worked with, even friends and family, had a point of view that was different from mine regarding a particular situation.

The Roman Emperor Marcus Aurelius, in his book *Meditations,* says "Nothing is good or bad until we judge it as such." I have found this to be true and apply it to all things in life now. My father's suicide, which I once saw *only* as a horrible, traumatizing event, I can now also see as a gift because of all the good that came after it. My family and I have grown closer; we've developed an incredibly deep level of empathy for others, especially those who they themselves are suffering in some way. All of us entered into some form of the helping profession within a few years of my father's passing. Service to others has been a large part of our lives for many years now.

It can be difficult at first to find a Guiding Healer; what is most important is the connection that you have with that person. There must be a deep connection, a feeling of being drawn to their energy and their teachings. Only then will you be most receptive and open, which is paramount to getting the most from the experience. Sometimes, you have to try a few different people before you find someone who is right for you. Support groups are a great place to start for some because they help you realize you are not alone, which is often how we feel while we are in pain, and you can get many referrals to different healers and professionals from those in the group.

Something to consider as well: we often seek out healers for our hearts, to help us overcome the emotional pain. What is most important during this time is to make sure all aspects of ourselves are being taken care of. That we are getting proper nutrition, taking in adequate amounts of water, staying away as best we can from toxic substances, influences, and people that will impede the process, and ensuring we are incorporating regular movement whether that means a daily walk or intense exercise. It has been my experience that incorporating all of these speeds up the healing process while helping us make the most of it at the same time. I would encourage you to find professionals who can help you with these and as always, check with your doctor before making any of these changes to your health.

The Second Path: Self-Healing

Self-healing involves retreating into ourselves in some way, usually through some form of short-term isolation, eliminating any and all distractions. We enter this stage when we take on the responsibility of healing ourselves through various practices such as deep isolation, meditation, introspection, yoga, silent retreats, etc. Now when I talk about any of these practices, I'm not saying we need to dedicate ourselves to them full-time, relinquishing all possessions, abandoning our jobs and our families, taking vows of silence and joining a monastery. No, I'm saying we should be incorporating the above practices as regular practices throughout our days as they provide fuel for the healing to take place.

Self-healing is nothing more than silencing the external and amplifying the internal, and being open and receptive to whatever comes up without judgment or attachment. This is, of course, the basis of a solid meditation practice, but just like the extremes above I talked about, you need not pursue formal, traditional meditation practices to engage in self-healing. In fact, sometimes when we pursue a formal discipline, it is easy to get caught up in attempting to perfect the practice at the expense of the purpose of the practice in the first place.

Self-healing can begin with a daily or even weekly nature walk where you do not bring along your digital device or any other form of distraction. Walk at non-peak times, if you can, on a trail that allows you at least 30 minutes to an hour of solitude where you can just pay attention to your thoughts, your internal dialogue and how you feed into them and make them worse. Then notice what happens if you don't actually feed into them, but allow them to just come and go. I like the idea of starting off with a nature walk as nature has been shown to be extremely beneficial for calming the mind and the body, helping us shut off the noise of the outside world, and reconnect with our deeper selves.

Yoga is also a great practice, as it involves both the mind and the body, which many including me believe is necessary for full healing to take place, as much of our past hurt is stored both in the mind and the body. I have made tremendous progress in my own healing of deep trauma by using both meditative style practices as well as body practices such as Yoga, Network Chiropractic Care (Network Spinal Analysis), Nature Walking (or as the Japanese refer to it, *Forest Bathing)*, Sensory Deprivation (Float Therapy), Massage, Energy work, and many others.

Self-healing can be where much of the healing takes place because only we can heal ourselves. True healing takes place internally, not by external means. For instance, we can seek Guided Healing for our pain, but if we are not open to it or we are not yet ready to accept the reality of our situation, then healing cannot take place. We must be able to take what we learn from the external and integrate it internally through introspection and internalizing before we can take another step toward transformation. We must *want* to heal. Receptivity precedes transformation.

It is important here to distinguish between retreating and running away. When we retreat into ourselves, pulling back from the rest of the world, we do so in an effort to silence anything that drowns out our inner voice and impedes the transformation process. We are eliminating anything that distracts us from our mission of introspection and spiritual healing; anything that will prevent us from making deep progress.

When we run away, we are running away from anything and everything that will amplify our inner voice. We run away from anything that reminds us of our feelings and the pain that has plagued us. We are avoiding feeling the pain. Running away is like sitting in your living room watching TV while completely ignoring the fact that your kitchen is on fire. Ignoring the fire doesn't extinguish it, and before you know it, everything else in the house, including the couch you're sitting on and even you yourself will be up in flames. In other words, just because you have disassociated yourself from the pain doesn't mean it's gone. It doesn't mean it's been dealt with or forgotten. And just like the fire that continues to rage, your body and your psyche will find a way for that pain to emerge at some point in the future, because you cannot run away from something that is inside of you. You cannot run from the pain you carry, that you have pushed deep into your psyche or stored in the tissue of the physical body. As JL Moreno famously said, *the body remembers what the mind forgets.*

So running away or ignoring what is going on inside is really not an option. Instead, we must get off the couch, grab the fire extinguisher and put the fire out while we still can, before it overwhelms us.

When we retreat into ourselves we have completely accepted the reality of our present situation and take the absolute personal responsibility to deal with and overcome it through full integration. We have seen the fire and realize we must act. Some people have a fear of this, but allow me to offer you the perspective of empowerment. Self-healing is an important part of this process because it is incredibly empowering. It restores our sense of control over the situation and we realize we are not as helpless as we thought we were. We are not a victim, though some may have been victimized; we no longer carry that label because self-healing makes us realize just how much control we have over our inner thoughts and feelings. What's more empowering, grabbing a fire extinguisher and saving your home and your loved ones or feeling unable to control the situation and succumbing to it? Going deep within to do the necessary work, to allow the pain to surface and fully discharge, is one of the most challenging, but liberating experiences of life. In my experience, there is no other way to full healing but to make this part of our practice, whether it is a standalone practice or in concert with the Guided Healing principle.

It is also important, I feel, to have a completely realistic understanding of what healing is and what it involves. I hear so many people talk about "putting the pieces back together again.". This, however, is misleading. Healing is not something we do so we can go back to who we were; we take the pieces and use them to create something even more beautiful than we had before. Transformation is about moving from one aspect into another. It is not about going back to who we were; this is impossible.

Let's use a mosaic for an example. A mosaic is a gorgeous piece of art. When you look at it from a distance, sometimes it can even look like a painting. But it's not. It's one big piece of art actually made up of tiny pieces of coloured tiles arranged to make a pattern. If you have ever looked at a mosaic up close, you will notice the pieces are not perfectly shaped. Or are they? They are jagged pieces of tile – so the piece itself is not "perfectly" square, in the way we would imagine it to be. But the piece *is* perfect in the sense that the exact shape and size is perfectly suited for its place in the mosaic – no other piece can take its place and give the artwork the same stunning beauty.

So this is our lives; not a sculpture created from one piece of stone but a beautiful piece of art created from broken, jagged pieces that have been perfectly arranged. Each experience we have, whether painful or joyful, we experience at the exact moment when it will be most beneficial and transformative for us. Like the tiles that compose the mosaic, its placement in our lives is perfect, despite what we may perceive as the jagged edges.

So building our own mosaic is what we are doing when we use self-healing as a method to transform ourselves into the state of fulfillment where we long to be.

Could you imagine an artist trying to put this mosaic together while there were tons of distractions around him? How difficult would it be to focus? To allow his muse to speak through him and show him exactly where each piece's proper place is? How long would it take for him to give up in frustration or give in to distractions and never fully complete the piece? How much more dimly lit would the world be without his work?

How much more dimly lit will the world be without your work, should you not take the time to eliminate distractions, be introspective, and allow the inner voice to provide you with the vision of how the pieces should go together in your own mosaic?

The Third Path: Healing Ourselves
Through Healing Others

This is the final stage of our healing process. We have gone from feeling like a helpless victim to once again experiencing our full power. We have taken our pain and turned it into a gift. Now, we can give that gift away. The beautiful thing about this is there is an unlimited supply.

Despite a painstaking search for the words to convey why healing others is so powerful for our own healing, those that follow will be woefully inadequate. So in some ways, you will just have to take my word for it until you experience it for yourself.

I personally believe it is difficult if not impossible for one to come as close as possible to having fully healed our spiritual wounds (I'm honestly not convinced we can ever fully heal to the point that whatever led us here no longer negatively affects us) without now using our pain to help others heal themselves.

I believe deeply that those of us who have walked the path of darkness have an obligation to shine a light for those who walk behind. We have an obligation to take all the wisdom and insight we have gained through our own process to help make it a smoother transition for those whose healing has just begun. We have something those who haven't gone through what we've gone through don't have; we have an unspoken bond. We are able to connect with others merely through our presence. We have an acute ability to recognize those who are walking the same path. And while each person's path has a different starting point, it would seem they are all leading to the very same fork in the road; with one way to fuller integration and the other way to deeper disintegration. We must stand at this fork, where we have stood before, to guide those approaching down the path to integration. Our world can no longer afford to leave this fork unmanned. And there are a few brave souls who go bravely and willingly down the path of deeper disintegration and shine their lights on those who walk it, illuminating the hell that lies at the end awaiting them, and guiding them back.

In my experience, I have found the greatest healers are those who they themselves have been touched as deeply by pain and trauma as those who seek their assistance.

I personally found that once I had gotten to a place where I felt healed, it became my relentless obsession to use what was once a source of unbelievable pain as fuel to help others progress through theirs. When I was finally guided to the right place at the right time and began working with clients, reflecting on our calls and what was said forced me even deeper into my own self-healing. The connections I established with callers during our short times together, and the insights I was able to guide them toward, were just as healing for me as they were for them.

I believe helping others heal is incredibly powerful because it normalizes the experiences that we have had. It normalizes them for others, and for us. So often when we experience crises we believe there is something wrong with us; that we aren't normal, and that no one else would handle it so inadequately. Working with those who are now where we once were is incredibly normalizing and validating of their feelings, and that can relieve a tremendous amount of self-imposed pressure. They feel lighter and, in that moment, so do we.

When we help others heal, we feel much more connected socially, but on a much deeper level. They can open up without feeling judged or ridiculed for doing so. They can unburden themselves and speak freely about their deepest, most personal fears and discomfort. There is so much satisfaction and fulfillment to be found in knowing that someone has placed such an enormous amount of trust in us to share such details. It renews our self-esteem. We see ourselves as contributors and humanitarians; we are no longer helpless or powerless or "bad." It provides us with even more (here comes that word again) *perspective*.

This is what I mean when I say you have turned your greatest pain into your greatest gift. Some of the most radiant, compassionate humanitarians are those who have experienced tremendous pain and adversity. They have used it to awaken new levels of empathy and compassion within so they could work to relieve the suffering in others.

Dr. Alberto Villoldo, in the documentary "Crazywise," states, "In the Shamanic traditions, you are not completely healed until you become the healer yourself. This doesn't mean you must heal others, it just means you must bring beauty, meaning, truth, and honesty into the world. That's when you become whole again."

In other words, healing others isn't necessarily realized by directly participating in another's healing process as a formal teacher, healer, or clinician. The way in which we live our lives and contribute to our humanity after the integration of our pain provides a model of possibility for those who come after us. We are living, breathing examples that we are not our past or our pain. When we are our authentic selves, when we allow our scars and our wounds to be exposed to the entire world without shame or inhibition, then we give permission to others to do the same.

What is most healing for others is not necessarily what is said during the interaction with a teacher or clinician, although that is of course impactful. It is looking into the eyes of someone else who can say, "I have been where you are, and I am here to show you that *you* can be where *I* am," not necessarily professionally, but emotionally, mentally and spiritually. This provides an unspoken reminder that healing is possible, and one does not have to live forever in pain.

This is truly what it means to heal ourselves through healing others.

Conclusion

Last year, I did something I never knew I was capable of: I sold my house and quit my full-time job, where I'd worked for the last 10 years, to start my coaching business. I spent the majority of the last year focusing on bringing myself back into a place of balance, inner peace, and good health, as my previous employment was extremely stressful and required me to spend a lot of time away from my family. It also involved shift work, which took a massive toll on my physical and mental health.

One thing I did to bring myself back to a better place was travelling. In November, I found myself in Kyoto, Japan in the middle of the Yasaka Shrine. There are several structures on the property, and right in the middle is a large wooden structure that had dozens of paper lanterns hanging from it. It was beyond beautiful. I must have stood there for 30 minutes completely mesmerized by the beauty of it, my mind was almost completely silent and I was just taking in the incredible energy of the area. It was definitely a moment of flow. It was a gorgeous fall evening and there were many people out, but it was by no means crowded. As I stood there, just meditating on what stood before me, people of all ages nearby were playing, laughing and just enjoying themselves. Normally, I would have found the laughter to be distracting at best and irritating at worse. But instead of getting irritated, I actually felt grateful. I had spent so much of my life surrounded by anger, negativity, criticism, trauma, fear, violence, and toxicity. I thought about where I was and what I was experiencing and how much better this reality was than the one I had been a part of in the past.

Then, something interesting happened. As I stood there, silently grateful to be surrounded by joy, laughter, and optimism, I took myself back to where it all began; the night my father died. I thought about all the Post-Traumatic Stress I had experienced, how it had brought me to my knees. I thought about my struggles with depression and anxiety and how I had lived in that for so long. I thought about how much fear and uncertainty about the future I lived in and how I thought it would never get better and that I would always be stuck, watching everyone else succeed while being left behind.

Back then, I recalled, I never could have even conceived of living with the kind of soul-freedom that has now become my status quo. I was so stuck in pain and suffering that it felt as though that would forever be my reality. I thought about the intense, painful, difficult work I had to do to get to where I am and how many times I thought about quitting or said, "this isn't working," but kept at it anyways. Then I thought about the incredible love, joy, freedom, that I had been surrounded by the last 7 months of being happily unemployed, the time I was spending with my girlfriend, my family and my friends, which I never thought I would have and never would have if I had given up and thrown in the towel every time I felt like it. Time most people would never become aware as being precious until they had run out of it for themselves.

Up until this point, while I was thoroughly enjoying my time in Japan, I was thinking more and more intensely about my business, how it would look, what I want to achieve with it and how I want to impact others and the world at large. I was so incredibly focused, feeling like there was no time to waste and needing to dedicate every free moment to building the empire. I am a perfectionist and high achiever, and I have a tendency to be very hard on myself, and feel like I'm not doing enough or building my business quickly enough. I'm still working to rid my subconscious of old programming no longer aligned with my new life.

This moment in the Shrine was most definitely a Self-Healing moment. I seized the opportunity to go deep inside and examine what was in there. It felt a lot like Life telling me, "Always remember the work you've done and be grateful for how far you have come while working towards what is next.".

We should never live in the past, or drive with our gaze in the rearview mirror. But I do believe we need to take regular times to examine how far we have come and really honour the work we have done on ourselves to get to the next level.

Things really do get better and you can create a life that's even better than you can imagine now, provided you do the work, working with a Guiding Healer such as a psychologist, a peer, a facilitated support group, a spiritual teacher, guru, or guide, etc. Or Self-Healing through meditation or yoga. Then getting to the place where you can Heal Yourself Through Healing Others, either directly by working with clients, or indirectly by contributing to humanity and the world in some way that uplifts people and helps them experience joy and love at a depth they've seldom if ever felt.

Life is challenging, yes, but all that means is that it is a never-ending opportunity for growth and success. No matter who you are, where you are, or what you have been through, you have gifts and talents to bring to the world. There is no shortage of opportunities to create a new life, a new future, and a new identity for yourself.

About 10 years ago I was doing some really intense inner work. I had a lot of anxiety around my relationships at the time; nothing seemed to be working. I was constantly ruminating, worrying, analyzing and dissecting. Part of my practice at this time was yoga and I was deep into it, going to classes about 4-6 nights a week. There was one particular instructor whose class I really enjoyed, because she focused on the traditional essence of yoga and put a lot of the attention on yoga's purpose in transcending our spiritual selves. After each class as we lay in our final shivasana pose, the instructor would read a page from a yogic text.

One evening after class, she uttered a phrase that has stuck with me and has helped me through the toughest of times: *no state of mind ever lasts.* Within a moment of those words leaving her lips, I felt a sense of total peace come over my mind and my heart. It was an incredible sense of relief that came with acknowledging the truth of her statement that this too shall pass. No state of mind, positive or negative, ever lasts. Neither do positive or negative experiences.

Whatever you're going through and whatever has led you to read this book, it won't last. I promise you. The trauma, the pain, the sadness, the disappointment; it's all come to awaken you. It has come to help you access a much deeper part of you. As soon as the negative emotions are processed and discharged, you will be left with a capacity to feel love, gratitude, peace, and joy on a deeper level than you ever experienced before. I speak from experience. It really is a gift. Never in my life did I imagine the place where I am now emotionally and spiritually even existed, let alone imagine I would achieve such an amazing state. And I'm just getting started.

As I sit here writing these last few pages watching the sun set from my living room, I am listening to an old radio show that kept me company back during the time I felt I had nothing and no one. As I listen to the program, I'm transported back to that time and how desperate I was to create something better for myself. It brought me so much hope, listening to the callers phoning in discussing their joys or their heartbreak with the host. It brought me so much comfort to know I wasn't alone in how I was feeling, and that there still was so much life for me to live. Now, here I am all these years later, listening to this same program with deep gratitude and contentment, because it was so worth doing the work.

So years from now, as you watch a beautiful sunset from your dream home, with that perfect person who found you at the exact moment they were meant to, how will you reflect on this part of your journey? I have faith that you will look back on this time with gratitude; gratitude for the strength you cultivated, gratitude for deepening your capacity to love, gratitude for believing in yourself enough to have faith that better things were ahead even if at the time your proof was limited.

Made in the USA
Middletown, DE
13 September 2018